THE BALL NEVER LIES
THE MENTALITY OF A WINNER

A PLAYBOOK OF
11 RULES TO LIVE,
LEAD AND LEAVE
A LEGACY.

Written in
English & Spanish
by

RAFA AMAYA
JOEY FLORES

Staten House
New York, New York
2025

Rafa Amaya | Joey Flores

Published by Staten House | New York, New York

Staten House

First Edition, 2025

ISBN: 979-8-89860-002-0 (paperback)

ISBN: 979-8-89860-007-5 (e-book)

ISBN: 979-8-89860-000-6 (audio)

Library of Congress Control Number: 2025914085

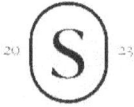

To our amazing reader:

You turn to the dedication expecting it to be for someone else. But not this time.

This one is for you, the one who is brave enough to live with purpose, lead with passion, and leave a legacy.

And for Joey's late grandfather whose quiet strength still echoes through it all:
Carlos Enrique Flores Gálvez.

When you move with purpose, the world around you moves too.

— JOE EDWARD BOYD

TABLE OF CONTENTS

FOREWORD

Dear Reader,

There are times in life when a single statement not only captures your attention but also freezes you in your tracks. *The Ball Never Lies* is one of those moments in my life. It's not a tired slogan or a catchphrase screamed from the sidelines. It's different. There is something more going on. Rafa and Joey are not borrowing the phrase; rather, they are coining it. More significantly, they're using it to develop something far larger.

They've taken this profound truth, one that lives at the very core of the game, into a leadership paradigm for how to live with clarity, compete with purpose, and lead with soul. This book is not just about what happens between whistles. It's about what occurs in the quiet moments when decisions shape character, when pressure shows preparation, and when you must decide who you truly are.

I've been involved in the beautiful game for many years, from representing Texas Lutheran University (TLU) as a student-athlete in the NCAA National Tournament to lifting a USL PDL National Championship trophy with the Laredo Heat. Today, I'm honored to coach at my alma mater, where I mentor student-athletes not only on the field but also in life. I've led our collegiate players on international humanitarian excursions to Guatemala in Central America, where soccer serves as a bridge between service, culture, and meaning. And through it all, every match, every practice, every difficult conversation, the same message has resurfaced: the game will never lie to you. It exposes your truth.

That's the heartbeat of this book. And that's why it is more important than ever. What makes *The Ball Never Lies* so effective is that it does not limit its appeal to players. This is not a book for a chosen group. It is for everyone. Whether you're a coach looking to lead with integrity, a young person pursuing a dream, a parent raising a leader, or simply looking for the next level, this book speaks to you. It meets you right where you are and provides you with the tools you need to move forward.

And the best part? It's inclusive. It doesn't matter about your background, gender, nationality, or title. Whether you grew up in a small town or a large metropolitan city, whether you've played the game or just appreciated its rhythm, this message applies to you. The 11 principles Rafa and Joey share are drawn from real experience. They've been lived, tested, and refined. These are not theories pulled from textbooks, they are truths earned through wins, losses, leadership roles, late nights, and comeback moments.

I believe in what this book represents because I've witnessed it in action. I've seen athletes use these ideas and transform, not only into better players, but also into better people. I've seen teams thrive after someone opted to lead from the inside out. The Rockefeller Foundation, *The Wall Street Journal*, and The United States Department of State have all recognized my work at the crossroads of sport, entrepreneurship, and community, but none of those honors match to the impact I've seen when people learn to live and lead with truth.

So, here's my challenge to you: don't just skim this book like it's another motivating read. Commit to it. Treat it like a preseason workout: with discipline, curiosity, and desire. Allow each chapter to challenge you, stretch you, and reveal something new. Allow it to improve your intuition, strengthen your vision, and stabilize your leadership under pressure.

This is not just a book. It's a playbook for life. What about the return on investment? Immeasurable. Because every new insight and change you make will have an impact on your family, team, business, and community.

And your purchase does more than just empower you. Ten percent of the net profits from this non-fiction book will benefit the Goal Impact Foundation, a reputable non-profit dedicated to developing leaders and creating safe, inspirational spaces for youth through education and sports programs. Every chapter you read helps to shape the next generation. Your advancement fuels their opportunity.

So read this book not just with your head but with your heart. Let it hold up a mirror. Let it stir something in you. And when the time comes, on the field, in a meeting, or in life, remember to bring these rules with you.

When everything else is gone and all that remains is your response to the moment, the ball always tells the truth. It is up to you to listen.

The ball's at your feet,

Jimmy Flores | *NCAA Coach, TLU Men's Soccer*

INTRODUCTION

Welcome Reader,

You did not come across this book by chance. You're here because something within you desires more, not just success, but truth. More depth. Increased clarity about who you are and how you lead.

We crafted *The Ball Never Lies* to fulfill that side of you.

This is not a book about tactics. It's a book about mental toughness, the kind that shows up under pressure, leads through hardship, and leaves a lasting impact well beyond the field. The kind of mindset that wins in life, not just in the final moments of a game.

Why this book? Why now?

Every era has a landmark, a moment that reminds us why the game is important. The FIFA World Cup is more than just a competition; it is a mirror. It reflects who we are, what we celebrate, and the type of leaders we develop, both on and off the field.

In a world eager for clarity, character, and connection, this book is a timely playbook. It is not hype. It's not a theory. It is a tried-and-true system designed for anyone who wants to lead with greater purpose, whether they're coaching a team, leading a business, mentoring youth, or simply striving to show up better in their daily lives.

These 11 principles don't just shape players, they shape people. And they invite you to play the long game: with heart, with conviction, and with legacy in mind.

The Origin Story

We coined the phrase *The Ball Never Lies* not because it was popular, but because it was missing. The world didn't need another trendy catchphrase; it needed a framework. A truth rooted in lived experience that applied not only to the game, but also to real life.

The Ball Never Lies is more than just words; it's a code for us. A code developed over years of playing, teaching, leading, and learning. The premise is that your habits, mindset, and decisions all indicate who you are. The way you train, respond under pressure, and lead when no one is looking is the true scorecard.

The work cannot be faked. You can't rush the soul. Eventually, the game, like life, will reveal the truth about how you show up.

This book turns that truth into a system: eleven rules, each associated with a jersey number and position and expressing a leadership concept intended to help you live it, lead it, and leave it as a legacy.

These aren't slogans. These are rules. They aren't concepts. They are codes, tested under pressure, across continents, and over decades of lived experience.

Meet Your Guides

Rafa Amaya provides what no one else can: the clarity and intensity of firsthand professional experience. He's competed at the top levels and coached on multiple continents. He coaches up-and-coming athletes as well as experienced veterans. His insights turn abstract concepts into grounded truths. He doesn't just talk to players; he speaks like one. His lens turns metaphors into muscle memory. His voice grounds this book to the reality of the game.

Joey Flores aka Bati provides balance. With a voice shaped by a lifetime of experience at all levels of the beautiful game, from federations and professional teams to universities and grassroots non-profits. He has witnessed how sports shape identity and how leadership leaves a legacy, from barrios to boardrooms. He adds depth and conviction, reminding us that what we learn in the game can change the way we live, love, and lead. He makes the game personal while conveying a universal message.

Together, we've created something timeless, not only for athletes, but for everyone. Not just locker rooms, but also classrooms, boardrooms, and living spaces. This is our framework, but it is now yours, too.

The 11 Rules of This Game

1. Master the Moment: Be still when others panic.

2. Defend Your Values: Protect what matters, even when it's unpopular.

3. Let Grit Speak Louder Than Ego: Show up with fire, not for applause, but for impact.

4. Stand for Something Stronger: Earn respect through consistency, not noise.

5. Be the Bridge: Connect with people, purpose, and play.

6. Outwork Your Circumstances: Show up with hustle that is therapeutic.

7. Dare to Create: Don't color inside the lines, redraw them.

8. Lead the Build-Up: Think three steps ahead and architect momentum.

9. Finish What You Start: Deliver with clarity, not chaos.

10. Make Greatness Contagious: Use your gift to elevate others.

11. Play for the People You'll Never Meet: Turn your pain into a platform.

Each rule is lived through both Rafa's and Joey's perspectives: Rafa from the fire of competitiveness and tactical clarity, and Joey from the soul of service, resilience, and transformational leadership. Together, they will help you lead with greater alignment, awareness, and action.

What You'll Gain

This isn't just a book to read; it's a training tool. It's intended to challenge, sharpen, and ground you.

Here's what you'll take away:

1. Develop the ability to lead through adversity by being cool and strong in difficult situations.

2. Develop mental discipline to master everyday habits and fundamentals.

3. Develop emotional and strategic intelligence to assist people through uncertainty.

4. Focus on character, purpose, and legacy to redefine success throughout time.

5. Lead by elevating others around you and leaving a lasting impact.

Who This Is For

The beauty of this book and the game is that it appeals to everyone. It doesn't care where you're from, what badge you wear, or if you've ever been on a field. *The Ball Never Lies* is not about the position you play, but about the position you assume in life.

Perhaps you're a coach seeking to create a long-lasting team culture. Maybe you're a young player looking for something more than stats. Perhaps you're a parent, a teacher, a mentor, or a leader who wants to assist people with compassion, clarity, and grit.

This book is for you.

It is intended for those who hold leadership positions in locker rooms, schools, boardrooms, and living rooms. For individuals who value process over perfection. For everybody who has ever overcome pressure, pain, or doubt and still decided to show up.

These 11 principles weren't learned in a seminar. They were earned in the mud, through struggle, humility, healing, and reinvention. We are not offering shortcuts. We are providing field-tested truth. If you're ready to lead with conviction, learn from hardship, and leave an impact, you've come to the perfect spot.

How to Use Your Field Notes

Each chapter concludes with a Field Notes graphic, which serves as a training ground rather than a recap. Whether you're a player, coach, parent, or leader, you'll get specific advice on how to live, lead, and implement each rule.

Begin with the part that pertains to your present role. Then return to studying the others. You will witness how truth transcends context.

Journal Prompts appear at the end of each section of the Field Notes. These are not simply supplementary reflections. They're your reps. Slow down. Sit with the questions. Write them down. Re-read them. That is where growth occurs, not just through reading, but also through reflection.

This book won't work unless you do. But if you do, we promise you'll see the results, both on the scoreboard and beyond it.

Playing With Purpose

As part of our dedication to making an impact, we're donating 10% of the net proceeds to the Goal Impact Foundation, a reputable non-profit that helps youth reach their full potential through education and sports.

When you purchase this book, you are not only investing in yourself. You're investing in kids who need a chance. You're helping to create fields, provide scholarships, and inspire hope. You're reading for something bigger.

How to Use the Visual Field Map

To help you fully understand the 11 principles in this book, we've included a visual diagram of the soccer field with each jersey number clearly marked in its position. This will serve as a reference throughout the chapters. Each rule corresponds to a specific position on the field, not only to teach strategy but also to reinforce a lesson.

Visual Field Map

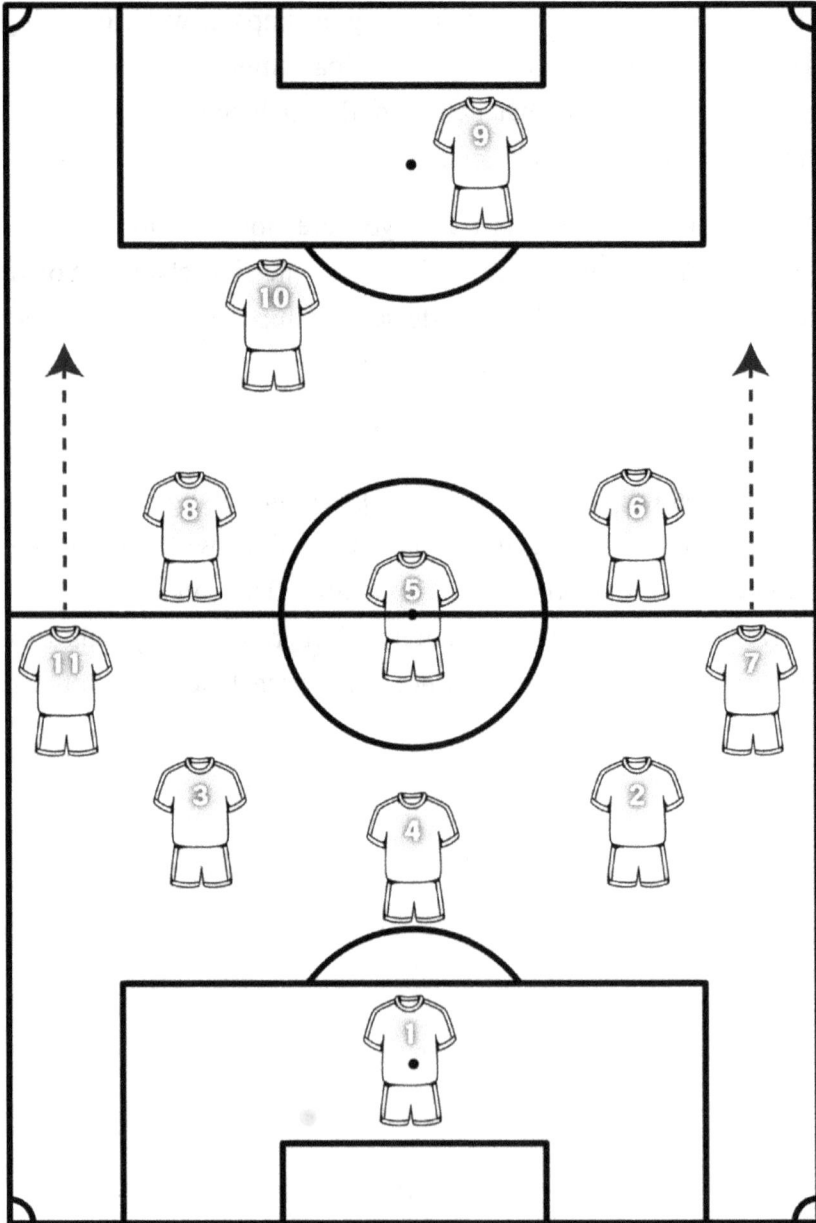

Your Role in This Movement

The Ball Never Lies is more than just a saying. It's a mindset. A metric. A movement. It signifies that your habits do not lie. Your preparation does not lie. Your daily effort tells the truth, even if the scoreboard does not. In this book, we share the guidelines we've followed as well as the lessons we've learned via hard experience.

Treat this as a training ground. Highlight it. Question it. Share it. Apply it. Use the field notes. Reflect on the prompts. Develop the muscle memory necessary for long-term success.

Let's get started.

Rafa & Joey

CHAPTER 1

Master The Moment

Introduction

Before the whistle blows, before the first pass is completed, and before a single tactic takes shape, presence is already at work. This chapter is about staying present in the moment, where pressure becomes possibilities and confusion becomes clarity. The goal is not only to get you ready for the game, but also to reset how you react to life's high-stakes situations. You'll discover how mastering presence, like the keeper who holds down their line, serves as the cornerstone for all other forms of leadership, resilience, and decision-making.

Matchday Mindset

"There's no such thing as a quiet player. Even when I was still, I had to speak louder than the storm." — *Rafa*

The last seconds of a match test more than just your reflexes; they also test your ability to deal with pressure.

The crowd is deafening. Teammates are scrambling. The striker is setting up for the final shot.

Now is not the time to overthink, panic, or shrink. This is when true competitors differentiate themselves.

It's not about saving or stopping; it's about being still. Regarding the internal reset. Own the moment before it owns you.

The Position's Energy

The goalkeeper wears #1 for a reason. They are the anchors, not only of formation but also of mindset. Their presence extends through the backline and forward into all phases of play. They are often the only one with a full view of the field, which makes their role not just merely reactive, but visionary.

A keeper's voice helps to organize chaos. Their calmness reassures defenders after mistakes. Their courage in one-on-one situations does more than only prevent goals; it also protects morale. They are the team's emotional thermostat. They see what others don't, speak when others hesitate, and bear a burden few comprehend. They are praised last but blamed first. And they still show up.

They operate in isolation yet must lead. They're the only position expected to be perfect while also being the last line of defense. Presence is essential, just like oxygen. Without it, the squad would suffocate under pressure.

However, presence does not imply appearing unfazed. It's about how to navigate chaos. It's not about denying fear; it's about knowing how to deal with it. It is not natural. It's been built.

When the game becomes more intense, you learn to breathe. You learn to see wider, slower, and smarter. You speak with the intention of being felt rather than heard. That is presence. And that is power.

Rule in Action: The Moment Rafa Froze Time

It was the semifinals in Bogotá. The heat pressed down, like a second jersey. The stadium erupted in cheers, fueled by momentum. Rafa's team was trailing 2-1. The ball kept slipping through their midfield like water, and the other team exuded swagger with each pass.

On the sideline, the opposing coach motioned for a switch. The winger peeled out wide. Their playmaker lined up to send a diagonal ball to the far post. The crowd rose with anticipation. Rafa, however, did not chase. He didn't sprint toward the ball like others might. He took five calm, peaceful steps forward.

When the pass was struck, Rafa was already there. He did not dive. He did not slide. He timed it precisely, picked it clean, turned up field, and launched a counterattack that changed the entire match.

The noise dropped. The energy switched. His teammates sensed the change, not because Rafa shouted, but because Rafa saw. His anticipation was not instinctive. It was presence. Earned through repetitions rather than games. Years of pressure circumstances and times of mental reset when everything demanded a reaction. That's the power of trained stillness.

Break It Down: What Presence Really Means

Presence is one of the most misinterpreted expressions of power, because it appears to be powerless.

It does not bark orders. It does not flinch in response to attention. It is quiet. Steady. Composed. It makes others feel secure, even when everything around is chaotic.

Presence is the capacity to control your breathing throughout adrenaline rushes. Make eye contact when others are looking away. Say less and mean more. It's all about timing, knowing when to speak and when to pause. It's about being aware of space, energy, and the emotional temperature of the room or field.

What looks like instinct is often just repeated, refined recognition. Great players and leaders don't merely react swiftly. They slow the game down. Presence turns seconds into space. Pressure into posture. It's built of quiet reps, in rituals people never witness. Those who master it not only survive but also alter difficult situations.

When you can hold yourself stable, you allow others to do the same. Presence does not demand to be followed. It just moves, and others follow naturally.

Rafa's Locker Room

In every elite camp I've coached, from national youth groups to professional trialists, one characteristic distinguishes the ones who thrive from the ones who fade: emotional control under pressure.

You can teach touch. You can improve your technique. What about presence? Presence goes deeper. Without it, the players unravel. I've seen technical standouts fail after a single wrong call. I've seen less gifted players remain on the field because they kept their composure. They made others feel safe. They converted tension into energy.

That is the player I want. That's the one teammates trust. Because they're not just present, they bring presence.

And yes, we train for it. I incorporate it into our sessions like I would any other skill:

- Maintain breath control during fatigue.

- Scanning during transitions.

- Maintaining eye contact during restarts and chaotic situations.

Presence must become muscle memory. If we don't incorporate it, we're building skill on shaky ground. Because great players don't just react; they read. They reset. When the moment comes, they rise silently.

Joey's Boardroom

My presence was once misinterpreted as rebellion.

I wasn't loud. I was not confrontational. I remained composed, which threatened the wrong people. They called it arrogance. They termed it defiance. But really, it was about clarity.

In rooms where power was fragile, I learned how to hold mine. Not by overpowering. By outlasting. While others battled to dominate the conversation, I concentrated on maintaining my posture, breathing, and holding the room without force.

My presence became a point of leverage. I didn't have to perform in global negotiations, tense board meetings, or quiet moments when everyone's attention was on me. I needed to align. I recognized that presence was more than just turning up like someone else. It was about consciously presenting my entire self.

That changed everything. I stopped overexplaining. I stopped apologizing for the energy I brought into the room. I began anchoring others by grounding myself.

When founded in reality, presence requires no label. It simply needs to be felt. And when it's genuine, when it's lived, it outperforms ego, noise, and any agenda in the room.

The Shift

We are frequently told that leadership belongs to the loudest voice in the room, that to be seen, you must speak first, quickly, and frequently. However, the fact is quieter and far more powerful: the person who breathes first, frequently leads best.

Presence is not a weakness. It's strategy. In a world that values urgency, presence is disruptive. It doesn't compete for attention, it keeps it. The players, coaches, and leaders who master presence do not panic in the face of pressure; instead, they make it wait. And it makes all the difference.

Conclusion

Presence sets the tone for everything else. It's not just about remaining calm under pressure; it's about being fully engaged, mentally sharp, and emotionally grounded. When you master the moment, you shift from survival to leadership mode. You become the calming force amid chaos, the anchor in which others may trust.

Now that you've grounded yourself, it's time to protect what's important. In the next chapter, we'll progress from goalkeeper to the center back. From mastering the moment to defending your values. This is where your allegiance is put to the test and where you draw the line.

CHAPTER 1 FIELD NOTES

IF YOU'RE A PLAYER

Every match presents pressure moments. Train for them. Practice "1-minute resets" after mistakes — stop, breathe, and re-anchor. Visualize chaos before bed and rehearse calm responses. Create a pre-game ritual that doesn't hype you up — but calms you down. Clarity outperforms adrenaline.

IF YOU'RE A COACH OR LEADER

Presence is contagious. Model it. In conflict, de-escalate with posture, tone, and timing. Build "presence checkpoints" into your practices — who holds eye contact, who slows the rush? Praise poise as much as performance. You're not just coaching skills. You're shaping state control.

IF YOU'RE A PARENT, TEACHER, OR MENTOR

Ask questions that invite awareness: "Where do you feel pressure in your body?" Then teach that calm is a skill. Show them how presence is power — even when unspoken. When kids see you reflect before reacting, they inherit that wisdom by osmosis.

JOURNAL PROMPTS

When was the last time you lost presence — and what did it cost you?

What situations tend to pull you out of the moment? Why?

What would it look like to lead from stillness this week?

CHAPTER 2

Defend Your Values

Introduction

Every squad needs someone who does not flinch. Someone who defends the flank, holds the line, does not seek credit, but never compromises. This chapter discusses that type of leadership. The kind that quietly fosters trust and aggressively defends values.

To defend your values, you must first identify what is most important to you and then live your life accordingly. This is not about being perfect. It's all about consistency. The right back does not make the headlines, but they lead the locker room. Not with noise, but with loyalty. With action. With presence.

You'll find that the most recognized leaders aren't necessarily the most popular; rather, they are the most principled.

Matchday Mindset

"The loudest trust is built from the quietest stops." — Joey

When the attack spreads along the wing, everyone realizes the danger, but not everyone responds.

The right back isn't waiting to be told. They resolve. They recover. They close it down. They don't need the crowd to cheer them on since they're too focused on ensuring the team's survival.

Defending your values is no different. When pressure hits, principles get tested. And those that lead with integrity don't preach their values; they live them. Each step. Every day.

The Position's Energy

The right back wears #2, not because they are the second-best, but because they are second-to-none in commitment. They guard the flank. They plug the gaps. They do the unseen work.

This position is loyalty, personified. They track back when others turn off. They maintain order even when the system gets stretched. They cover for others without keeping score.

They don't chase the spotlight; they protect the mission. As a result, they develop into the type of teammate that others rely on when everything is at stake.

Values function in the same manner. They are not for performance. They are for protection. If you don't defend them, no one will.

Rule in Action: Joey's Quiet Stand

It was not the championship. It was not even televised. But it was the type of game that exposed everything.

Joey's squad was young and energetic but lacked discipline. The team captain barked orders without earning trust. When a midfield error resulted in a breakaway down the right side, all eyes went forward, except Joey's.

He saw the rotation. He saw the winger cheat. And while the rest of the team froze, Joey sprinted. Covered two players. Blocked the shot.

No stat line. No celebration. Just a nod from the coach and a quick shift in the team's energy. From that moment on, they played tighter. Not because Joey told them to, but because he showed them how.

Trust is not loud. It's earned in the little decisions. It's what happens when you show up, lock in, and make the play that counts, whether anyone sees it or not.

Break It Down: What Integrity Really Means

Integrity is not about being perfect; it is about being faithful. It is important to present yourself consistently, whether people are observing or not. Whether or not the lights are on, or the locker room is quiet.

To defend your values, you must define them. What are your non-negotiables? What lines are you unwilling to cross, even if it means losing popularity, playing time, or applause?

Integrity is the result of repeated decisions. It is built around tiny sacrifices rather than grand gestures. It's not about what you say in interviews, but about how you treat others in silence.

And when people know what you stand for, they don't have to question who you are under pressure.

Rafa's Locker Room

I've coached players who could talk a good game, but I trusted the ones who didn't have to.

Want to know who earns minutes? The right back who does not complain about the assignment. The one who runs when their legs are gone. The one who holds shape even when others gamble.

Loyalty isn't just mindless obedience. It's about being clear. Players who understand and embrace their roles lay the groundwork for the team's success.

In my sessions, I look for:

- Who sacrifices without a spotlight?

- Who covers for others without keeping score?

- Who speaks through action?

Those players? They run locker rooms. They defend culture. They earn trust and make everyone else safer simply by being on the pitch.

Joey's Boardroom

Early in my career, I realized the consequences of remaining silent on important issues. I believed that playing it safe would protect my path. But I quickly discovered that silence could feel like betrayal when values are at stake.

I've sat across the table with power brokers who wanted me to compromise. Dilute the message. Play politics. Smile through the shade.

But I discovered something important: being liked is not synonymous with being trusted.

So, I quit pleasing. And began protecting the truth, even if it cost me business, followers, or favors.

When I started defending my values, not with noise but with consistency, the proper people started showing up. They prioritized alignment over acclaim. And I became someone others could rely on to be there when it mattered.

The Shift

In a world concerned with attention, protecting your principles may be the most daring move you take. Loyalty doesn't trend. Integrity doesn't get likes. However, when the pressure builds, and it always does, it is not noise that holds the line. It's about conviction.

We've been sold the idea that popularity equals power. That being liked is equivalent to being trusted. But trust is earned in the unglamorous moments: when you support a teammate after a mistake, when you speak the truth in front of an audience, and when you act in alignment even if it costs you anything.

The players who defend with intention, who do what is right without being praised, affect the entire game. Off the field, things are no different. Because the strongest lines are not drawn in the sand. They're etched in values. And when those values are visible, they echo longer than any applause. You don't have to yell to stand firm. You just must stop what others let slide.

Conclusion

To defend your values is to define your legacy. Instead of slogans, use standards. Not with performance, but with presence.

Right backs do not chase the ball; instead, they guard the flanks. And leaders do not chase approval; instead, they protect the truth.

In the following chapter, we shift from defense to defiance. From safeguarding what matters to demonstrating that grit outperforms ego. Because stepping up with fire, and no need for applause, could be your greatest strength.

J.

CHAPTER 2 FIELD NOTES

IF YOU'RE A PLAYER

Leadership starts with loyalty. Ask yourself: what do I stand for when no one's watching? Make your non-negotiables clear. Be the teammate who covers without complaint, recovers without blame, and plays with integrity — even when it's not rewarded. Trust is your real stat line.

IF YOU'RE A COACH OR LEADER

Set the tone with standards, not slogans. Model the values you want echoed. Protect the culture — especially when it's inconvenient. Praise players who sacrifice quietly. Correct with consistency, not emotion. Conviction creates clarity. And clarity builds championship environments.

IF YOU'RE A PARENT, TEACHER, OR MENTOR

Talk about values openly. Ask: "What do we believe in — and what does it look like in action?" Reward consistency more than charisma. When young people see you stand firm in what matters, they learn that courage isn't always loud — it's steady. And contagious.

JOURNAL PROMPTS

When was the last time you stood for something — even if it was unpopular?

What are three non-negotiable values that guide your decisions?

How can you model loyalty and conviction this week?

joeyflor.es

CHAPTER 3

Let Grit Speak Louder Than Ego

Introduction

Every team has a player who isn't flashy but is always the first to tackle. The one who doesn't talk big but plays big. This chapter is about that spirit. The underestimated warrior. The one who allows their grit to speak for itself.

To lead with grit means to overcome ego. It means showing up with fire, not for attention, but for something deeper. The left back does not demand the ball. They expect respect. And they acquire it by doing the hard, dirty work, the unnoticed reps that make a difference.

You'll realize that true winners are motivated by purpose rather than fame. In a world obsessed with credits, your best move might be to show up without needing any.

Matchday Mindset

"Grit is the quiet engine that drives the loudest victories."
— Rafa

The left back understands that their name will not be in the news. But they show up, nonetheless. Every match. Every minute. There is no fanfare, only fire.

They sprint back when others jog. They slide when others hesitate. They get up one more time, even though no one is clapping.

That is grit. It does not wait for applause. It plays with a purpose. Because ego desires to be seen. But grit wishes to serve.

The Position's Energy

The left back wears #3, which is often overlooked and underappreciated. But without them, everything falls apart.

They are the wall no one anticipates but on which everyone depends. They do the work no one volunteers for. They recover, reset, and resist.

Their power? It is quiet. It's enduring. It is consistent. They pursue discipline rather than highlights. Others play for cameras, but they play for the crest.

That's what makes them dangerous and dependable. Because every locker room, every field, and every organization requires someone who prioritizes contribution over credit.

Rule in Action: Rafa's Street Lesson

Before contracts, stadiums, and pro kits, there were cracked sidewalks and worn-out cleats.

Rafa grew up in a supportive environment where each match was a test and an honor. Your reputation was founded not on style, but on who got back up. He recalls a game on an improvised field, with no lines, no referees, just pride.

He took a hard hit and went down. Laughter followed. But so did Rafa. He got up. Dusted off. Did not swing. Did not pout. He played harder. He won every duel after that.

Nobody applauded. But everyone noticed.

Because grit does not want attention. It wins respect. Quietly. Completely.

Break It Down: What Does Grit Really Mean

Grit is not the same as noise. Grit is the willingness to do the difficult thing rather than receive easy praise. It stays after when no one is looking. It's doing the reps that don't go viral but leave you unshakable.

Grit says: "I'm not here for credit. I am here to contribute." Ego inflates. Grit endures. Ego seeks the reward. Grit lives in the process.

And the funniest thing? Those who let grit lead frequently win in the long run, not just trophies, but also trust. Because everyone remembers the person who consistently showed up.

Rafa's Locker Room

When I build a back line, I do not begin with flash. I start with fire. I look for a player who gets stepped on and doesn't retaliate, instead plays harder. The one who closes down a winger and then applauds the center back's clearance. The one who doesn't seek praise but shifts the entire line.

You want to lead? Show up without being asked. Sacrifice without keeping score. Outrun, outlast, and out-hustle.

During training sessions, I observe:

- Who wins 50/50s without talking about it?

- Who confidently resets after making mistakes?

- Who motivates the team when they are at their lowest point?

That is the type of player who survives, not because of ego, but because of perseverance.

Joey's Boardroom

I never based my career on charisma. I based it on consistency.

Early on, I learned to quit pursuing praise and instead pursue meaning. I was hardly the loudest person in the room. I took the meeting that no one wanted. The one who delivered even when nobody applauded. The one that stayed longer, asked more in-depth questions, and consistently followed through.

I was overlooked. Undervalued. Until I was not.

Because grit has a way of appearing on the scoreboard of legacy. Not in likes. But in terms of impact. The business world rewards those who close deals. However, legacy favors finishers who never had to be seen to serve. That's the path I chose, and I don't regret a single step.

The Shift

In a world that values flash, letting grit take the lead may be the boldest move you make. Highlights trend. Hype sells. But when the lights fade, as they inevitably do, it's not flair that gets you through. It's fire.

We've been taught that visibility means value. That if no one sees it, it does not count. But the ones who last? They're the ones who work hard without being noticed. Who show up when it is inconvenient. Who create their reputation through reps rather than reels.

Players that play for a purpose rather than for credit, shape the culture. Off the field, things are no different. Because the most effective leaders do not always receive the most attention. They're the ones who remain standing when the applause stops.

You do not have to perform to be remembered. You simply need to show up when it's difficult and keep showing up after that. That is not a weakness. That is grit. And that is the foundation of legacies.

Conclusion

To let grit speak louder than ego is to lead from a different perspective. Hunger for contribution rather than credit.

Left backs don't need to make headlines. They ensure that the scoreline survives. Leaders that act with grit rather than ego influence the culture.

In the following chapter, we move deeper into the core. From silent grit to the spine of belief. Because standing up for something greater could be the next test of your leadership.

CHAPTER 3 FIELD NOTES

IF YOU'RE A PLAYER

Stop chasing the spotlight. Chase the standard. Hustle on the plays no one watches. Get up when no one helps you. Let your effort speak louder than your ego. Grit doesn't beg for approval — it earns trust through consistency, resilience, and sacrifice.

IF YOU'RE A COACH OR LEADER

Start celebrating the grind. Reward the players who do the work nobody sees. Grit is teachable — but only when it's valued. Set the tone by praising toughness, effort, and accountability. When grit becomes culture, ego gets benched.

IF YOU'RE A PARENT, TEACHER, OR MENTOR

Help young people understand the difference between being seen and being solid. Ask: "What's something hard you kept doing — even when no one noticed?" Show them that real impact doesn't need applause. It needs purpose. And practice.

JOURNAL PROMPTS

When was the last time you chose the hard road over the flashy one?

Where are you showing up for others — without needing recognition?

How can you lead this week by letting your grit speak for you?

CHAPTER 4

Stand For Something Stronger

Introduction

Every team has its anchor. The one who holds the middle when the storm hits. The player who refuses to fold, even when things go bad. This chapter discusses that type of leadership: the core. The spine. The one who can be felt without being seen.

To stand up for something stronger than yourself, you must rise rather than react. You don't simply show up; you hold the line. Center backs aren't in the game for show. They're in it to protect what counts. They do not explain but rather lead by example.

You'll discover that the leaders who build cultures aren't the ones pursuing credit; rather, their clarity becomes contagious. Because when things fall apart, everyone turns to the center.

Matchday Mindset

"Strong teams are built on someone who won't bend." — Joey

When the game gets physical, the opposing team plays dirty, and the referee loses control; the center back does not panic. They plant. They take up position. They protect.

They don't yell at the chaos. They keep it quiet. Not with words, but with presence. With action. With belief.

To stand for something stronger is to become the team's spine. Not through noise, but through non-negotiables. You do not need the armband to lead. You only need conviction.

The Position's Energy

The center back wears #4, not for flash, but for foundation. They serve as the system's backbone, providing a protective shield when all else fails. Their timing disrupts goals. Their positioning saves games. Everyone is held together by their beliefs.

They can view the field clearly. They command with caution. They absorb pressure without passing it on. When the midfield scrambles and the attack stalls, the center back is still there, organizing, adjusting, and standing firm.

Their strength is not loud; rather, it is long-lasting. And in leadership, that means everything. Because when the front-line tires and the sideline becomes quiet, it is the spine that keeps the team standing.

Rule in Action: Joey's Quiet Defiance

In a playoff match against a top-seeded team, Joey's squad was younger, smaller, underappreciated. The opposing team attempted to rattle them with hard fouls, trash talk, and theatrics.

Midway through the second half, tension erupted. A fight almost broke out. Coaches yelled. Fans surged. But Joey did not move.

He stepped through the disorder. Did not react. Simply reset the line. He told his teammates, "Play your game." And they did.

They won the match. Not because they had better talent. But they stood for something more powerful, calm over chaos. Purpose over pride.

That moment was not flashy. But that was everything.

Break It Down: What Strength Really Means

Strength is not the same as noise. It's about conviction. It stays rooted while others are spinning. It is leading when there is no spotlight, no comfort, and no guarantee.

To stand up for something stronger, you must first establish what you will not compromise on. You must lead during the storm, not only when the skies are clear.

The strongest leaders do not demonstrate strength. They practiced it. In routines. In rituals. In reflection. They don't always speak first, but when they do, it counts. And when the going gets tough, they become the calm others lean on.

Rafa's Locker Room

When I scout center backs, I look for more than simply tackles. I am looking for temperament.

Can they lead without shouting? Can they stay composed when the referee misses a call? Can they organize the line, not merely with their words, but also with their actions?

I look for players who:

- Stay calm in stressful situations.

- Adjust formation without waiting for instructions.

- Encourage teammates while anchoring the back line.

A center back is more than just muscle; they are the defense's mind. They do not fold. They do not fade. They do not fake.

They stand. And that strength changes everything.

Joey's Boardroom

I've been in rooms where I wasn't the oldest, loudest, or most powerful person. But I stood for something. That was ultimately what mattered the most.

During one negotiation, I felt pressed to look the other way. "Just sign it," they said. "No one will know." But I knew. And I could not.

I spoke up. Not to perform, but to protect. Not for my ego, but for my integrity. I lost the contract. But I gained something more powerful: self-respect. And, eventually, better rooms.

Standing up for something stronger does not guarantee you victory in every situation. But you always win in front of the mirror.

The Shift

In a world obsessed with charisma, standing steady may be the most underestimated type of leadership. Visibility receives applause. However, when pressure peaks and everything is at stake, allure becomes irrelevant. It is your spine.

We are taught that strength must be obvious. However, actual strength remains even when the system cracks. It keeps the room stable as everyone else moves around. It does not demand attention; rather, it earns trust.

The players who anchor belief, not for clout but for clarity, are the foundation of any great culture. This is also true in real life.

Those who hold the line even after the crowd has dispersed, have the greatest lasting impact.

Being a leader does not need you to push your way to the front. You simply must maintain your footing when others fall. That is not resistance. That is resilience. And it's what people remember after the dust settles. Because when pressure comes, and it will, charisma does not hold the line. It's about conviction.

Conclusion

To stand for something greater is to be more than a player. More than a professional. It's to be a presence.

Center backs do not flinch. They do not flex. They do not follow the noise. They uphold the standard and by doing so, keep the team together.

In the next chapter, we move to the middle of the pitch. From holding the line to building the bridge. Because true leadership is defined by the connection of people, purpose, and play.

CHAPTER 4 FIELD NOTES

IF YOU'RE A PLAYER

Hold your line — even when the pressure rises. Great defenders don't just clear the ball — they clear the noise. Let your poise steady the team. Lead with composure, not commentary. Respect isn't earned by flexing. It's earned by standing firm when others fold.

IF YOU'RE A COACH OR LEADER

Make clarity your compass. Teach players to lead from the back — not just with tackles, but with trust. Build your system on repetition, care, and conviction. Honor the quiet anchors. Because when pressure hits, it's the spine — not the slogans — that holds.

IF YOU'RE A PARENT, TEACHER, OR MENTOR

Talk about what it means to lead without applause. Ask: "What's a moment where you stayed calm when others didn't?" Help them see that true leadership doesn't shout. It shows up, holds steady, and shapes others — by standing for something stronger.

JOURNAL PROMPTS

When did you last stay steady while others lost control?

What core belief helps you lead under pressure?

How can you be someone others trust when the game gets chaotic?

CHAPTER 5

Be The Bridge

Introduction

Every team needs a translator who makes the chaos make sense. The one who ties the back to the front, the line to the concept, and the play to the purpose. This chapter is about that leader, the bridge-builder. The person who not only passes the ball but also conveys confidence, rhythm, and clarity.

To be the bridge means to stabilize the system. Not in flash, but in flow. Holding midfielders do not compete for headlines. They play for harmony. They lead by connection, not command. And that type of leadership is not always obvious, but it is always necessary.

You'll learn that the most influential leaders aren't usually the loudest; they're the ones who make everyone else feel 100% more certain, simply by being present.

Matchday Mindset

"A good pass moves the ball. A great one moves belief." — Rafa

The holding midfielder does not need to wow the fans. They must win the moment between the lines. They stop danger before it arrives. They scan, pivot, and simplify.

They don't chase the game; they shape it. They make the complex look clean. They complete the necessary tasks before anyone notices. When a team frays under pressure, they become the glue. Bridges do not demand attention. They provide it for everyone else.

The Position's Energy

The #5 represents the pitch's pulse. The holding midfielder sees both sides and knows both languages. They connect the defense and the attack. The structure and spontaneity.

They do not try to do everything; rather, they aim to make everything work. Their presence allows others to play more freely by taking risks and attack more boldly. They know the bridge is behind them.

It is not about being the star. It's about being the foundation behind the star. And in every great team, whether on the field or in life, it requires someone to hold everything together.

Rule in Action: Rafa's Guiding Thread

Rafa was coaching a U17 academy match. His team was full of talent but lacked coordination, causing them to become shaky.

Their opponent could sense vulnerability, making them feel more confident, high pressing and hungry.

Rather than changing formation or replacing the flashy player, Rafa pulled his holding midfielder aside. He did not discuss tactics. He discussed presence.

"Play simpler. Speak more. Let them breathe."

The kid did not score. Didn't assist. However, he touched the ball more than anyone. One-twos. Shoulder checks. Covered gaps. Calmed nerves.

By full time, the team had found its rhythm and its leader.

Break It Down: What Stability Really Means

Stability is not rigid; it is fluid structure. It is knowing when to push and when to pause. It's reading the room and then resetting it.

Bridge-builders don't need credit but thrive on connections. This allows them to calm chaos, and make people feel more confident and connected.

It's not about filling every role; it's about empowering those that are in the role. When the bridge is strong, it provides everyone with an opportunity to soar. That type of leadership is sensed among one another, rather than shown.

Rafa's Locker Room

When I train holding mids, I don't look for the flashiest, or even the fastest. I want to know: Who organizes? Who anticipates? Who communicates?

The best fives make others better without making a scene. They:

- Reset the tempo after a turnover.

- Speak calmly and clearly when others tense up.

- Fill in spaces others forget.

I teach them to scan the field as an announcer would read the score board. Because it isn't only about where the ball is; it's also about what the team needs in the next play. Bridges do not need praise. They need clarity. And that clarity wins games.

Joey's Boardroom

In diplomacy and business, I'm rarely the one making headlines. However, I've frequently been the one building bridges behind the scenes.

The person who translated between departments. The one who kept egos steady throughout negotiations. The person who saw the early warning signs before they broke the system.

That's the work of a connector. You aren't doing it for attention. You are doing it for alignment. You don't need the spotlight since you're holding the structure. When you build them right, the systems you touch do not collapse; instead, they carry.

The Shift

In a world that glorifies stars, the bridge is frequently forgotten. Visibility earns likes; connection earns trust. And when a team begins to falter, it is not flash that keeps it together. It's function.

We have been taught that leadership means taking center stage. The most effective leaders, however, are not constantly in the spotlight. They're the ones in the middle, keeping everything steady, scanning, and serving.

The players who create rhythm, restore calmness and make others better. They do not need credit because their influence speaks through everyone else's success. This is also true in real life.

You don't have to lead loudly to lead effectively. You only need to keep others connected when the game gets scattered. That is not a trivial task. That is essential work. And it is what ensures the longevity of teams and legacies. Impact does not always announce itself. Sometimes, it simply makes the entire system work.

Conclusion

Being the bridge brings and holds everything together. Not for credit, but for continuity. Holding midfielders do not seek the moment. They shape it. They are the present that connects the past with the future. They lead the team without chasing the ball.

In the following chapter, we move from connection to commitment. From bridge to engine. Outworking your circumstances is the next test of who you are and where you are going.

J.

CHAPTER 5 FIELD NOTES

IF YOU'RE A PLAYER

Bridge the gap. Be the voice that calms, the pass that connects, the presence that centers. Holding mids don't need the highlight — they need the heartbeat. Reset the rhythm when things speed up. Cover when others drift. Keep the team ticking with trust and tempo. Leadership isn't always a sprint — sometimes it's a steady pulse.

IF YOU'RE A COACH OR LEADER

Honor the glue. Celebrate the ones who organize, who simplify, who don't chase credit but create cohesion. Build your practices around transitions — not just in play, but in energy. Watch who leads from the middle — with clarity, communication, and care. Because when everything feels unstable, bridges bring flow.

IF YOU'RE A PARENT, TEACHER, OR MENTOR

Teach the power of quiet contribution. Ask: "When have you helped others succeed without needing attention?" Show young people that leadership isn't always about being seen — it's about being someone others can lean on. Stability is a gift. And the ones who offer it are often the ones who lift the most.

JOURNAL PROMPTS

When did you last make someone else's job easier — just by how you showed up?

What does being a 'bridge' look like in your daily life?

How can you lead from the middle this week — with calm, clarity, and connection?

CHAPTER 6

Outwork Your Circumstances

Introduction

Every team needs an engine, someone who never stops running, thinking, or pushing. The one who keeps the entire system running without being told. This chapter focuses on that relentless force. The player who not only fills space but also fuels it.

Outworking your circumstances is to convert hustle into therapy. It's not about being flashy; it's about remaining committed. Box-to-box midfielders clock in. Every play. Every moment. Every inch. They never check out.

You'll discover that the actual power isn't where you start, but in how you regularly show up. Because effort does not merely influence performance. It shapes beliefs.

Matchday Mindset

"The work you do in silence will one day speak for you."
— Joey

The box-to-box midfielder is everywhere. Breaking up plays in the backfield. Driving transitions in the middle. Supporting front-line attacks. They create their own moments rather than waiting for them.

They are the first to press and the last to fade. They cover mistakes without complaint. They work not for glory, but for advancement. When everyone else starts to slow down, they shift into another gear.

That's what separates them. Not just their talent, but their tempo.

The Position's Energy

The #6 wears invisible armor. Built from habits. Hardened by consistency. They are not looking for accolades, but rather for ways to improve.

Their job? Everything. Nothing showy. They win the ball. Make the pass. Start the press. Track the runner. They hold standards others forget. They show up when it's boring, brutal, nasty and ungrateful.

This position demands endurance, discipline, and grit. Above all, it requires conviction, not in hype, but in hard effort. Because the engine does not have to be seen. It simply needs to run.

Rule in Action: Joey's Miles of Meaning

There was a time when Joey trained alone, with no team, coach, or camera. Just cones on cracked pavement. Sunrise runs through quiet neighborhoods. Hundreds of touches. Reps in quiet.

No one watching. No one clapping. Just work.

Years later, in an international friendly match, Joey found himself in a tight midfield battle. Fast opponent. High stakes. Limited space. But Joey did not panic. He pressed. Won the ball. Spun out. Launched a counter.

That play didn't start on that pitch. It began in the miles no one saw.

Because hustle, when aligned with purpose, becomes something sacred.

Break It Down: What Hustle Really Means

Hustle is not noise. It's a commitment. It's setting your alarm when no one's checking. It's choosing reps over rest. It's moving from motivation to discipline.

True hustle is a mindset, not a phase. It is what turns talent into trust. Not just in yourself, but in those around you.

When you outwork your circumstances, you don't just climb; you elevate everything you touch.

Rafa's Locker Room

I tell every young player this: your work ethic is your signature. Not your skill. Not your status. Your work.

When I analyze a box-to-box midfielder, I'm watching for:

- Who keeps going after a missed pass?

- Who tracks back when they're tired?

- Who lifts others with their effort?

This position does not allow you to excel in only one area. It's about executing a magnitude of duties well and repeatedly. It's about being consistent.

I don't care how much talent you have. I can't build around you if you don't put in the effort. But if you do? I'll trust you every time.

Joey's Boardroom

The best leaders I know did not achieve their success through shortcuts. They outworked their pain, their background, and through noise.

Early in my career, I kept showing up in places where I wasn't expected to be, let alone influence. But I kept preparing. I kept learning. Kept serving. That is what kept me there.

Work ethics isn't just about grinding; it's also about alignment. I didn't try hard to prove my worth. I worked hard because what I was creating mattered.

And when your effort matches your purpose, people remember. Not because you talked about the grind, but because you made your work undeniable.

The Shift

In a world obsessed with outcomes, effort might be the most radical expression of belief. Flash draws attention. But consistency builds trust.

We've been taught that grind is loud, but the true version is silent. It shows up when no one claps. It leads while no one is looking. It outlasts talent because it is based on something more than applause.

Players that lead with effort do not need to post about their progress; they live it. Off the field, things are no different. The leaders who change cultures are those who make discipline contagious.

You do not need to prove yourself to everyone. All you must do is prove to yourself that the standard is sacred and act accordingly. Because when life tests your limits, and it will, it's not hype that carries you. It's hustle.

Conclusion

To outwork your circumstances means to lay a solid foundation that no one can shake. It is to act as a leader. By digging. By deciding that not your limitations, not your critics, not even your past, can outrun your efforts.

Box-to-box midfielders don't get many breaks. However, they create breakthroughs. Not with hype but with hustle.

In the following chapter, we change from work ethic to creativity. From effort to expressiveness. Because daring to create is the next big step, and risk, in being a memorable leader.

CHAPTER 6 FIELD NOTES

IF YOU'RE A PLAYER

Stop waiting for perfect conditions. Outwork them. Show up when it's hard, not just when it's hyped. When others coast, commit. When no one's watching, train anyway. Your discipline is louder than any highlight. Consistency isn't sexy but it's what separates workers from wishers. Let your hustle become therapy. Let your work become worship.

IF YOU'RE A COACH OR LEADER

Make effort the expectation, not the exception. Build sessions that reward grit over glamour. Track habits, not just stats. Praise follow-through, not just flair. Honor the players who grind without applause, they're the ones who raise the floor. Teach that hustle isn't just about energy, it's about alignment with something bigger.

IF YOU'RE A PARENT, TEACHER, OR MENTOR

Talk about the sacredness of showing up. Ask: "When have you done something difficult and kept doing it without being pushed?" Remind young people that consistency is more powerful than charisma. That doing the work, even when it's inconvenient, builds the inner muscle no one can see, but everyone feels.

JOURNAL PROMPTS

When was the last time you showed up — even when you didn't feel ready?

What habit are you building that no one claps for — but matters?

Where in your life can you turn effort into a sacred act this week?

CHAPTER 7

Dare To Create

Introduction

Every team needs a spark, someone who lights up the field with rhythm, danger, and even rebellion. The one who does not wait for permission to play freely. This chapter is about that energy. The player who turns a simple touch into art, a tight space into a statement, a quiet game into a moment no one forgets.

Daring to create means taking the initiative to use one's imagination. To innovate under pressure. To believe that creativity is more than a choice; it is an obligation. Wingers don't ask where the line is. They draw new ones.

You'll discover that creativity isn't fluff. It is fuel. Leaders who discover their own uniqueness can often discover the uniqueness of others.

Matchday Mindset

"Creativity isn't chaos, it's courage in disguise." — Rafa

The winger dances on the edge. Wide space. Tight pressure. A wall of defenders challenging you to play it safe.

But the great ones don't fold; they rise. They cut inside while others stay outside. They dribble past doubt. They try things that were not in the playbook.

They know expressions are risky. But so is playing small. What if they fail? They will try again. Because wingers do not wait for opportunities to make an impression. They create it.

The Position's Energy

The #7 does not always follow the script; instead, they remix it. The winger's role is not just to defeat defenders. It is to cause discomfort. To change the tempo. To get the game going.

They stretch the field. Inject energy. Force the opposition to adjust. They may not touch the ball frequently, but when they do, it changes the rhythm.

They live on the edge. Reason being this view gives them the advantage to see what others cannot. That perspective can be quite powerful if perceived with intention.

Creativity isn't only about being flashy. It's about the vision that is called intuition. This is also called bravery. The winger's role is to challenge predictability and invite possibility.

Rule in Action: Rafa's Disruptive Dribble

Rafa was coaching a U15 game. It was considered boring with predictable passes and no risks being taken. Without warning, one of his wide players with frustration and bravery took a chance. Nutmegged his mark. Switched pace. Curled in an unexpected cross. Goal.

The sideline exploded. Not because it was flashy, but because it changed the tone. The whole team was lifted.

After the game, Rafa did not praise the move. He praised the mindset. "You did not wait for the game to come to you. You went and found it."

That is what wingers do. They make courage contagious.

Break It Down: What Creativity Really Means

Creativity is misunderstood. It's not reckless. It's a responsible risk.

It's visualizing what isn't there yet. It is trusting your intuition when the script doesn't fit.

True creativity is not about going viral; it is about getting deeper. It's about believing in your own unique way of solving problems. And allowing others to see possibilities through your play.

Creative leaders build what did not exist before. They disrupt, not to destroy, but to evolve.

Rafa's Locker Room

I teach my wingers they can disrupt rhythm but not trust.

So, I watch for the following:

- Who dares in the final third?

- Who tries again after failing?

- Who makes the field bigger for others?

Creativity is more than just stepovers. It's about making decisions. It's bravery under pressure. The best wingers do more than just express themselves; they uplift. Because when they create something new, they invite the entire team to experience a new dimension.

Joey's Boardroom

I used to dilute myself down to fit the space. Then I realized my uniqueness was one of my values.

In pitches and strategy sessions, the most significant breakthroughs occurred when I stopped replicating what had previously worked and began inventing with my own voice.

Innovation is not about creating something shiny. It is about solving problems. It's about speaking up when others won't. Attempting what others haven't.

The biggest deals I've ever landed didn't come from following the rules. They came from reinventing them with the courage to believe in my ideas. Even when they seemed unusual, this inspired others to do the same and believe in themselves.

The Shift

In a world that rewards formulas, creating your own could be your greatest act of leadership. Predictability receives approval. However, creativity generates movement.

We've been taught to play it safely, to color within the lines. But safe does not scale. And lines do not liberate.

The leaders who dare to innovate do not need applause; they need space. Space to try. To fail. To learn. And then try again. While ego seeks certainty, creativity thrives in discovery.

You do not have to be fearless to innovate. You simply need to be true to your spark. Because when you move with originality, real, raw, and disruptive innovation, you don't simply play the game. You change it.

Conclusion

Daring to create entails accepting that your uniqueness is both a gift and a responsibility.

Wingers don't simply run fast. They run free. They don't just defeat defenders. They bend expectations.

In the next chapter, we will transition from the spark to the structure. From creativity to orchestration. Because seeing the entire play, and creating it with purpose, is what comes next.

CHAPTER 7 FIELD NOTES

IF YOU'RE A PLAYER

Creativity is courage in motion. Stop waiting for permission. Take the risk. Try the move. Trust your difference. Wingers weren't made to play it safe — they were made to spark something wild. When the match gets predictable, you get unpredictable. That's leadership too. Not by control — but by imagination. Let your expression ignite the team.

IF YOU'RE A COACH OR LEADER

Don't just coach execution — coach expression. Build environments where new ideas are welcome and mistakes are seen as growth, not failure. The most creative players often feel the most misunderstood — until someone gives them space to fly. Nurture those sparks. Structure should support creativity, not suppress it. If the game is art, let your players paint.

IF YOU'RE A PARENT, TEACHER, OR MENTOR

Celebrate the weird. Honor the kid who dreams big and colors outside the lines. Ask: "What's something only you would have thought to create?" Show them that leadership isn't always logical — sometimes it's lyrical. That boldness doesn't always shout — sometimes it shines. Creativity is a seed. Protect it, water it, and let it grow into something that outlives you.

JOURNAL PROMPTS

When was the last time you created something — just because it mattered to you?

What part of your identity do you sometimes hide — but could be your superpower?

How can you lead with imagination and boldness this week?

CHAPTER 8

Lead The Build-Up

Introduction

Every team needs an orchestrator, the one who turns movement into meaning. The one who views the game as a whole, not just a collection of events. This chapter focuses on that leader: the architect in the middle. The one who doesn't just react to the play; they create it.

To lead the build-up is to set the rhythm. To influence how people feel before they recognize it. Central midfielders don't wait to be instructed where to go; they tell the game what's coming. They don't chase plays; they create patterns.

You'll realize that true leadership is more than vision. It's about structure. Because seeing the future is meaningless if you can't influence it.

Matchday Mindset

"You don't control the match with magic. You control it with rhythm." — Joey

The central midfielder has eyeballs everywhere. They don't need the spotlight; they need the plan. They take the first touch with purpose. They play through pressure. They make the field feel bigger and the game feel slower.

They know when to hold. When to press. When to unlock.

Because the number eight doesn't just play the game. They conduct it.

The Position's Energy

The #8 represents the nerve center. The translator. The tactician. What's their job? Connect everything. Connect the lines. Solve the problem in motion.

They are the first to organize following a turnover. The first to notice a third pass before the first one is even completed. They change the tempo. Reset the shape. Create outlets.

Great central midfielders aren't emotional; rather they're accurate. Nonetheless, they still bring heart. Because it takes courage to hold the middle.

Their strength is not in flair, but in foresight. And in any system, someone must think three steps ahead. That's the eight.

Rule in Action: Joey's Tactical Pivot

In a high-stakes match, Joey's team was pressing but stuck. The final third was congested. No space to break through.

So, Joey dropped deep. Called the switch. Baited the press. Then sprayed a diagonal ball that broke two lines and set up a goal.

After the game, the coach didn't talk about the pass. He spoke about the pause.

Joey saw not only the play, but also its timing. That is what orchestrators do. They don't only move the ball. They shift the moment.

Break It Down: What Orchestration Really Means

Orchestration represents leadership in action. It is strategic planning without freezing. It involves reading patterns and creating new ones. It is not enough to have vision; it is also necessary to put it into action.

Great playmakers don't simply see what's there. They sense what's coming. They read pressure like weather. They build shape with every touch.

Orchestration is calm. Calculated. Creativity with constraints. It's knowing how to maintain tension until the moment is right and then releasing it with precision.

And when done correctly? It doesn't only alter the play. It changes the tempo, stance, and belief of the team.

Rafa's Locker Room

When I develop a central mid, I do not begin with passing. I start with perception.

Who scans before the ball arrives? Who knows when to speed it up or slow it down? Who organizes others while executing?

Here's what I look for:

- Who positions before receiving?

- Who can lead without barking?

- Who focuses on building rather than breaking?

I teach them to think like conductors. Because when you lead the build-up, your role is more important than any statistic. You influence the way the team breathes.

Joey's Boardroom

In every venture I've led, I've had to be the link between vision and system. I am not the flash. I am the flow.

In one project, the creative team had brilliant ideas. The operations team had rigid systems. We kept missing deadlines, until I stepped in and mapped a new framework that accommodated both.

That's when I realized that being an orchestrator isn't about having the loudest voice. It's about coordinating timing, trust, and tools.

Leadership entails more than simply identifying problems. It is all about designing what holds. The best leaders I know are thinkers who build, not just dreamers who drift.

The Shift

In a culture fascinated with huge moments, being the architect of movement might be your most subtle and profound legacy.

Hype generates noise. Orchestration facilitates growth.

We're told to pursue impact. However, true impact is built one brick at a time, rep after rep, pass by pass. It is not a reaction; it is rhythm. It is not hype; it is harmony.

Those who lead the build-up do not always get the credit. But they get the culture going. They make connections seem unavoidable.

You do not have to call every shot to lead. You only need to create a system where others can shine. Because when pressure strikes, as it inevitably does, those who have built well do not panic.

They pivot. They play on.

Conclusion

To lead the build-up means to be in control of the plan. Those who read the play before it unfolds and who ties vision to action, and action to results.

Central midfielders don't chase the moment; they create it. They create lanes for others to run through. They make structure seem like movement.

In the next chapter, we move from orchestration to execution. From shaping the play to finishing it. Because seeing the opportunity is one thing. Closing it? That is where legacy lives.

CHAPTER 8 FIELD NOTES

IF YOU'RE A PLAYER

Lead the rhythm. Be the one who sees the play before it happens. Don't just follow — orchestrate. Scan the field, move with intention, pass with purpose. Your job isn't to steal the spotlight — it's to shape it. Great #8s don't just play well — they make everyone else play better. Think ahead. Act early. Let your vision become the team's momentum.

IF YOU'RE A COACH OR LEADER

Develop pattern recognition and decision-making — not just technical drills. Build sessions around anticipation, flow, and structure. Ask: who thinks three steps ahead? Who can pivot with purpose? Celebrate the ones who make systems work smoother. Great leadership isn't just reaction — it's architecture. Make space for the players who build the build-up.

IF YOU'RE A PARENT, TEACHER, OR MENTOR

Teach the value of vision. Ask: "Where do you see things others miss — and how can you act on it?" Help young people understand that leadership isn't always loud or flashy. Sometimes, it's thoughtful. Strategic. Steady. Show them how vision paired with structure can create freedom — not restrict it. Let them practice being the planner behind the moment.

JOURNAL PROMPTS

Where in your life are you reacting instead of architecting?

Who in your circle needs your clarity and steady presence right now?

What system, routine, or structure could you build this week — that helps others thrive?

CHAPTER 9

Finish What Your Start

Introduction

Every team needs a finisher, someone who not only dreams of goals but delivers them. The one who steps up when the stakes are high and the scoreboard still needs changing. This chapter is about that type of leader: the closer. The one who moves not merely with ambition, but with precision.

To finish what you started, lead with clarity. To take responsibility for the outcome rather than merely the idea. Strikers do not hesitate. They don't hope. They prepare. They place.

You'll learn that legacy is based on precision, not potential. The world does not reward what you start. It remembers what you've finished.

Matchday Mindset

"Finishing is not a moment. It is a mindset." — Rafa

The striker sees the opportunity before it arises. They understand the run, the weight, and the strike. There's no panic, only presence.

In the box, there is no space for doubt. There's no time for second guessing. Great attackers don't just shoot. They choose. They scan. They strike.

Execution is not about talent. It's about timing. And timing? That must be trained.

The Position's Energy

The #9 represents the heartbeat of ambition. The finisher. The person who turns buildup into breakthrough.

Their value isn't in how many touches they get, it's in what they do with the right one.

They read the backline. They create half yards. They move purposefully. When the time comes, they do not blink; they bury.

Being a striker isn't about chaos. It's about clarity. Only preparation, repetition, and belief can provide that level of precision.

Rule in Action: Rafa's Clinical Close

In a knockout match, Rafa's team was awarded a penalty in stoppage time. Tie game. One shot. One moment.

Rafa did not rush to the spot. He walked. Took a breath. Blocked out the noise.

The keeper guessed early. Rafa stayed calm. Slot it low and clean. Game over.

What looked like instinct was years of repetition. What felt like courage was really clarity.

You do not finish big moments by accident. You finish them because you have done it a thousand times in silence.

Break It Down: What Execution Really Means

Execution is not about pressure. It's preparation. It's not just about wanting the moment; it's about being ready for it.

Great finishers prepare for turmoil. They practice control. They trust their habits more than the hype.

Execution involves discipline. It's about making decisions. It is the mindset that says, "If this moment comes, I will be ready."

You gain that trust not just from others, but also from yourself.

Rafa's Locker Room

When I coach strikers, it doesn't matter if they miss. I care about how they miss. I am concerned about how they recover.

I look for:

- Who takes the same shot in training like it is game day?

- Who rebounds mentally after a miss?

- Who moves with belief rather than bravado?

Finishing is not flashy. It is focused. You don't need ten chances if you train like you only have one.

The best nines do more than just shoot. They study. They sharpen. They show up in the moment because they've shown up in the trenches.

Joey's Boardroom

Everyone in business appreciates a good concept. However, very few people finish.

Early in my career, I had a pitch that sparked excitement. But excitement does not close deals; execution does. I learned to be the one who delivered. The person who followed through. The one who ensured that the concept lasted beyond the pitch deck.

That is what finishers do. They are responsible for the outcome. They lead with purpose. They don't just talk about vision; they achieve it.

Finishing is not about perfection. It's about presence. About having the guts to finish what others only start.

The Shift

In a world full of starters, finishing may be the most radical leadership move you make. Ideas are everywhere. Execution? That's rare.

We've heard that dreaming big is enough. However, vision without completion is only noise.

Those who finish build trust. They anchor belief. They do more than just create movement; they also seal it.

You do not need to be perfect to lead. You only need to be the one who delivers. Because when the pressure rises and the window narrows, it is not the intention that matters. It's the impact.

Conclusion

To finish what you started, declare that your word is valuable. That your work is grounded in action.

Strikers do not chase hope. They seek outcomes. They move decisively. In doing so, they remind all of us that completion is where confidence begins.

In the next chapter, we step into a new dimension. From individual delivery to collective elevation. Because making greatness contagious is the next test. Not of skill, but of spirit.

J.

CHAPTER 9 FIELD NOTES

IF YOU'RE A PLAYER

Be the one who finishes. When others hesitate, decide. When the moment gets tight, stay clear. Strikers don't just shoot — they sharpen. They rehearse the run, the touch, the finish until it becomes second nature. Clarity kills doubt. So does preparation. Let your movement be intentional and your mindset unshakable. Great finishers don't just find chances — they create closure. Make the last step count.

IF YOU'RE A COACH OR LEADER

Prioritize execution. Build a culture that doesn't just dream well — but delivers. Teach players to close plays, close reps, close responsibilities. Ask: who follows through with focus? Who brings precision to pressure? Execution is a habit, not a highlight. Celebrate the ones who bring things to completion. The ones who finish strong, not just start fast. Because in every mission, there comes a moment where someone has to close the door. Teach them to be that someone.

IF YOU'RE A PARENT, TEACHER, OR MENTOR

Model the power of follow-through. Ask: "What's something you started — and what did it take to finish it?" Show young people that starting is easy — but finishing is earned. Let them see that grit doesn't just mean working hard. It means completing what you commit to. Teach them to move with decisiveness, not delay. And remind them: finishing what matters builds confidence that can't be coached — only lived.

JOURNAL PROMPTS

What's something important you started but haven't finished — and why?

Where in your life would more clarity help you take decisive action?

How can you show up this week as someone who finishes what they start?

CHAPTER 10

Make Greatness Contagious

Introduction

Every team needs a maestro, someone who not only plays the game, but enhances it. The player who inspires, sharpens, and improves others around them. This chapter is about that kind of leadership: the artist-engineer. The one who uses vision not to impress, but to inspire.

To make greatness contagious is to lead with generosity. Instead of hoarding your talent, spread your confidence. Attacking midfielders do more than just take the last shot; they see the pass before anyone else does. They are not just dominant. They design.

You will discover that true greatness is not demonstrated through solo performances. It is provided by the ripple effect you cause on others.

Matchday Mindset

"True maestros don't just dazzle, they direct." — Joey

The number ten plays for more than just glory; they also play for flow. They penetrate tight defenses. They draw pressure to create space. They make brilliance feel like a team sport.

When the tempo needs to be changed or the atmosphere lifted, the ten steps in. Not with noise, but with nuance. Not with ego, but with impact.

They don't simply play their position. They raise everyone else's.

The Position's Energy

The #10 is a conductor in cleats. They orchestrate, disrupt, and deliver. They are the link between the builders and the finishers. The heartbeat of imagination.

Great tens don't just take the spotlight; they redirect it. They see what others miss. They move into spaces no one else notices. They pass in ways that change posture, not simply possession.

They understand that their gift is not merely to shine, but to ignite. Because when you're in the middle of the play, the goal isn't to be seen. It's to help others be seen more clearly.

Rule in Action: Joey's Unselfish Assist

In the cup final, Joey had a chance to shoot. The defender was off balance. The keeper was leaning. But in a split second, he noticed the winger rushing in, wide open.

Joey did not hesitate. One-touch layoff. Tap-in. Goal.

The crowd cheered for the goal scorer. But the bench knew. The coaches knew. The moment was created, not claimed.

After the match, a teammate said, "That's why we trust you. You always see us." That's the power of contagious greatness. It multiplies confidence and elevates trust.

Break It Down: What Greatness Really Means

Greatness does not hoard talent; rather, it honors it. And the best way to honor it? Share it.

Contagious excellence is based on humility. It shows up to empower rather impress. It plays a long game. It knows that the best legacy is not being remembered for what you did, but for how you influenced the growth of others.

When you make others shine, you will not fade. You are the leader.

Rafa's Locker Room

I teach my tens that their mission is to illuminate, not only create.

So, I watch:

- Who turns pressure into an opportunity for someone else?

- Who creates space and recognizes the assist?

- Who energizes the team when they feel down?

Great tens don't just run plays; they read emotions. They sense momentum shifts. They raise the level without raising their voice. And the team rises with them, because their greatness is never just theirs.

Joey's Boardroom

In every arena where I've led, the most effective leaders were not those with the impressive résumé. They were the ones who enhanced the room's intelligence, calmness, and creativity.

I build systems that provide others with a platform, even if it means stepping back. I share the microphone. I transfer the credit. I enjoy mentoring people who will eventually outgrow my guidance.

True achievement is not a pedestal. It is a ladder. Each step you create for someone else? That's the actual scoreboard.

The Shift

In a world concerned with going viral, making others visible could be the most revolutionary act. We've been taught to protect our edge. With contagious greatness, the edge is shared. It doesn't fear being replicated; rather it thrives on it.

Some of the most prominent leaders aren't always the ones who make the final play. They are the ones who started it but willingly allowed someone else to receive the final play. You don't need a highlight reel to make history. You only need to believe that success multiplies when you give it away.

When the world sees you helping others, they will feel your greatness the most.

Conclusion

To make excellence contagious, rise and invite others to join you. It is to share without shrinking. To serve without craving the spotlight.

Attacking midfielders don't just move the ball. They influence belief. They use their gift to unlock others.

In the final chapter, we widen the lens one last time. From contagious greatness to legacy. What you give to people you will never meet is the ultimate confirmation of who you truly are.

J.

CHAPTER 10 FIELD NOTES

IF YOU'RE A PLAYER

Use your gift to lift the group. Make the extra pass. Celebrate the assist. Spotlight the unsung. True greatness doesn't hoard — it shares. Don't just chase the moment — create moments for others. The most valuable players aren't just difference-makers. They're difference-multipliers. Your legacy won't just be in what you did — but in who got better because you were there. Let your presence elevate the whole pitch.

IF YOU'RE A COACH OR LEADER

Redefine leadership as amplification, not attention. Build teams that honor contribution over credit. Ask: who makes others more confident? Who brings out brilliance in teammates? Great leaders develop leaders — not followers. Celebrate the pass before the pass. The movement that opened space. The energy that lifted the room. Contagious greatness is a culture. And it starts with leaders who make generosity the norm — not the exception.

IF YOU'RE A PARENT, TEACHER, OR MENTOR

Model legacy through generosity. Ask: "What's a way you've helped someone shine — without needing the spotlight?" Show young people that real success includes others. That leadership isn't just about being followed — it's about lifting. Let them see you praise behind the scenes. Share what you've learned. Share what you've earned. Because when young people grow up in environments where success is shared, they learn that greatness grows stronger when it spreads.

JOURNAL PROMPTS

Who have you helped grow — and how did it impact both of you?

What's a gift you have that could lift someone else this week?

How can you lead by spotlighting others — not just yourself?

CHAPTER 11

Play For The People You'll Never Meet

Introduction

Every team needs a player with soul, the kind that moves like a seasoned veteran and leads like a legend. This chapter is about that rare leader: an expressive force who reminds us that greatness is more than just winning. It's about meaning.

To play for the people you'll never meet is to live with a legacy in mind. It is to use your presence not to perform but to liberate. Left wingers do more than merely widen the field. They stretch our thinking. They remind us that the goal isn't always to score but sometimes, it's to pay it forward.

You'll learn that true legacy does not end with you. It begins with whom you help become freer.

Matchday Mindset

"Legacy is not a look back. It's a reach forward." — Rafa

The number eleven does not play for applause. They play for impact. They move with rhythm and rebellion, expressing what can't be explained.

They chase more than goals. They pursue justice. Joy. Possibility. And when the game tries to shrink, they make it bigger. For everyone. They don't simply leave their mark. They make others more visible.

The Position's Energy

The #11 represents artistry with urgency. Left-wingers break patterns and inspire belief. They build out of chaos and invite others to follow. They're bold. Brave. Soulful.

They don't play for the moment. They play for the meaning inside the moment. They don't just lift their team; they lift their people. Their ancestors. Their future audience.

To them, every move is more than just technical. It is spiritual.

To play from this place means remembering that your story is not just yours. It's a symbol of someone else's freedom.

Rule in Action: Rafa's Quiet Dedication

Years after retiring from the game as a player, Rafa coached a youth player who reminded him of himself; raw, unpolished, full of talent and emotion.

The kid did not have much. No gear. No guidance. But he had a spark. Rafa saw it. And showed up for him, every session, ride, and moment.

That player had no idea that the previous mentors of Rafa had done the same for him. Although, he didn't have to because of legacy. A legacy that served as a chain of beliefs being passed down quietly.

Rafa knew that one day that same youngster would eventually show up for someone too. Not because he is told, but because of what Rafa has shown him.

Break It Down: What Legacy Really Means

Legacy isn't loud. It's enduring.

It's not about how many people remember your name; it's about how many people can walk freely as a result. It doesn't matter what you win. It's about who you uplifted, through your presence, platform, and pain.

When you play for the people you'll never meet, your leadership is eternal. You stop pursuing credit and begin influencing futures.

The best part? You do not need a stage. All you need is purpose larger than yourself.

Rafa's Locker Room

I tell my left wingers, the way they play, will tell a story. They don't have to say anything.

So, I ask:

- Who moves with meaning?

- Who plays for something deeper than stats?

- Who leads like a great leader once led them?

The best wingers I've ever coached didn't just want the ball. They wanted to make people feel. That is power. That is legacy. That's how you become memorable, not for what you did, but the purpose of what you did it for.

Joey's Boardroom

For years, I believed legacy meant being remembered for the memories I left behind. I now understand it's the feeling of being valued that I left behind within others.

My proudest moments did not come from deals or speeches. They came when someone said, "You helped me believe again." or "Because of you, I didn't give up."

My platform was never mine. It was up to me to utilize that platform and transform it into a foundation I could use to lift and amplify. Also, to remind others that their story is still sacred. Even when it has previously been silenced.

I now speak not just for myself, but for those who were not given the opportunity or allowed to. My hope is that eventually, someone will do the same for me.

The Shift

In an era concerned with labels, playing for people you'll never meet could be the most radical type of leadership.

We are trained to pursue likes, clout, and applause. However, legacy lives in quieter places, in the lives touched by what we gave, not what we kept.

Some of the most legendary players didn't just score or put points on the board themselves. They liberated. They gave others a reason to believe again. Not because they were perfect, but because they made space for others to rise.

You don't need a statue to leave an impression. You simply need to love out loud and live for those who have not yet arrived.

Conclusion

To play for the people you'll never meet, is to become a bridge between pain and purpose. It's to use your story to unlock someone else's strength.

Left wingers don't only dribble. They deliver spirit. They don't only play to win. They play to remember and be remembered, correctly.

And this is how you finish your book. Not with loudness, but with soul. Not with ego, but with offering.

In every play. In every step. In every moment.

May your story not only set yourself, but someone else, free.

The Ball Never Lies

CHAPTER 11 FIELD NOTES

IF YOU'RE A PLAYER

Play with soul. Let your story show in how you move. Compete for more than just points — compete for purpose. Express what others are afraid to say. Your legacy won't be measured only in stats, but in the hearts you shift by being fully seen. When you turn pain into fuel, joy into freedom, and pressure into poetry — others follow. Don't just play for the crowd. Play for the quiet ones watching — the ones you'll never meet, but who'll never forget how you made them feel.

IF YOU'RE A COACH OR LEADER

Teach players to lead from within. Build teams that move with meaning. Ask: Who plays like their story matters? Who plays like someone paved the way for them — and is paving it for someone else? Celebrate the ones who bring soul to the field. Remind your team: leadership isn't just about results — it's about reverberation. When your why is big enough, your impact doesn't stop at the sideline. It echoes in players you may never coach, because your influence already reached them.

IF YOU'RE A PARENT, TEACHER, OR MENTOR

Model legacy through story. Ask: What's a moment in your life that gave others permission to be more free? Remind young people that vulnerability is strength, and that being seen — truly seen — is not weakness, but a gift to others who are still hiding. Share how someone else's courage shaped you, and let your own story become a stepping stone. Because when youth see that pain can become purpose, and story can become service, they stop shrinking — and start standing taller.

JOURNAL PROMPTS

Who's someone you've never met, but who inspired you to be braver — and why?

What part of your story might help someone else feel seen or strong?

How can you move this week with legacy in mind — for people you'll never meet, but whose lives you can still impact?

CONCLUSION

Recap of *The Ball Never Lies* Principles

As we reach the final whistle of this journey, let's take a look back. Focusing on the 11 soul-rooted rules that have guided us from the back to the frontline, and from the inner effort to outer legacy:

1. Own the Moment (Goalkeeper): You learned that presence is power. Being grounded, still locked in, transforms pressure into clarity. It separates competitors from champions.

2. Defend Your Values (Right Back): Loyalty isn't loud. It's lived. You don't win trust by talking, you earn it through consistent action, even when no one's watching.

3. Let Grit Speak Louder Than Ego (Left Back): This rule reminds us that hustle doesn't ask for applause. It just shows up. Again, and again. The uncelebrated reps become your reputation.

4. Stand for Something Stronger (Center Back): In a world full of noise, clarity is strength. Leadership starts when you hold your ground with conviction, especially when others fold.

5. Be the Bridge (Holding Mid): True leadership connects. It's about making others feel more confident, less chaotic,

and more seen. When you hold the middle, everyone else can move freer.

6. Outwork Your Circumstances (Box-to-Box Mid): Your story may begin in struggle, but your grind defines your ending. Greatness isn't given but earned. One silent rep at a time.

7. Dare to Create (Right Winger): You weren't born to fit the template. This rule urged you to disrupt, to express, and to turn your difference into your edge.

8. Lead the Build-Up (Central Mid): Vision without structure is just a dream. True orchestrators build the rhythm that others can run with. They don't chase the play, they shape it.

9. Finish What You Start (Striker): Ideas are everywhere. However, the world remembers finishers. This rule calls for decisive action, practiced precision, and execution that inspires trust.

10. Make Greatness Contagious (Attacking Mid): Use your gift to lift others. The real magic of leadership isn't in being the best, it's in making everyone around you better.

11. Play for the People You'll Never Meet (Left Winger): Legacy isn't what you keep, but what you give. When you move with meaning far beyond your name, your story becomes a platform for others to rise.

Reinforcing the Core Themes

These 11 guidelines are not simply rules; they represent a methodology for soulful leadership. Together, they create a framework based on three enduring themes:

- Conviction: You lead not by force, but by clarity. Whether you're defending values, finishing strong, or building structure, conviction keeps you grounded in moments that test you.

- Contribution: From connecting plays to lifting teammates, greatness is measured by what you can provide. True leaders don't chase credit, they create culture.

- Cause: Each rule becomes more powerful when it's tied to something bigger than yourself. That's where real transformation begins, when purpose meets performance.

Daily Application: How to Live the 11 Rules

1. Play With Purpose

Set an intention every day that aligns with one of the 11 rules. Whether it's daring to create, showing up with grit, or simply being fully present, play on purpose.

2. Rewatch the Tape

Reflect Weekly. Where did you lead well? Where did you hesitate? Use the rules as a mirror, not for guilt, but for growth.

3. Build in Public

Allow others to see how you've integrated the rules. Whether you coach, parent, mentor, or compete, demonstrate what it means to live with conviction, contribution, and purpose.

4. Anchor in the Why

When it gets hard (and it will), remember why you're doing it. The rules are a compass, not a checklist. And your legacy is defined by how you maintain alignment when life gets messy.

Final Thoughts: *The Ball Never Lies*

Do not perceive this as a book, but a mentality to show up. A system for building your legacy, one principle at a time. These rules are not intended for easy games on, nor off the field. They were designed for high-stakes moments. For the pandemonium. For a comeback. For the cause.

Power in Practice

Leadership starts in the repetitions. The ones nobody sees. And each time you reset, recover, and reengage, you develop habits that will make your presence felt, long after you leave the field.

Positivity in Motion

Being a winner does not imply toxic positivism or sugarcoating setbacks. It's about valuing power over pity. Purpose above passivity. It is about going through life with energy that liberates rather than just motivates.

Legacy in the Long Game

Your legacy is not your highlight reel. It's called the ripple effect with the space you provided. The belief you passed on. The team you lifted. That is what people will remember and what will last.

A Call to Lead Loud and Live True

These 11 rules originated on the pitch, but they continue to exist beyond it. They're for the parent teaching resilience. The coach shaping character. The artist disrupting norms. The leader playing for a cause beyond applause.

So, take these rules. Live them. Share them. Embody them.

Let them echo in your actions and ripple through your reach.

Because *The Ball Never Lies* and neither does your legacy.

Here's to your next step.

Make it count. Make it louder. Make it contagious.

END NOTES

Recognitions Cited

1. Department of State United States of America, *Secretary's Award for Corporate Excellence*, (U.S. Embassy Guatemala City, Guatemala, 2013)

2. The Wall Street Journal, *Digital Publication*, https://www.wsj.com/articles/SB100014240527023040961045792386909825151198, 2013)

3. The Rockefeller Foundation, *3S Awards Global Sourcing Council*, (New York, New York, 2012)

AFTERWORD

As we reach the final pages, we're not closing a story, we're opening a deeper chapter within you. *The Ball Never Lies* isn't something we just wrote. It's something we've lived, lost sleep over, trained through, and built our lives around. As this book reaches your hands, we find ourselves inside a powerful pause. One meant for reflection, reconnection, and renewed conviction.

This book has always been more than a creative pursuit. It's a return. Return to the fields where our love for the game first ignited. A return to the locker rooms where we discovered the meaning of team, trust, and tension. A return to the values whispered to us by mentors, coaches, elders, and the game itself. The work you've just read is born of that invisible thread. One that ties the game we love to the people we are, and to the lives we've committed to shaping beyond the final whistle.

We didn't write this because it was trendy. We wrote it because it was necessary. Every principle and every insight is fingerprinted with our real-life experiences. From muddy pitches and packed stadiums to quiet nights where doubt sat heavy but never won. From federation strategy rooms to moments on the sidelines as fathers, brothers, and coaches; this is the work of a lifetime, not a single season.

The 11 principles in this book aren't borrowed or imagined. They're authentic. In pressure. In failure. In grit. They came to life through late nights, early mornings, and that familiar ache in your soul when you know you're being tested, not by an opponent, but by life itself. These truths weren't handed to us, they were earned. And now they're yours.

While writing, we pictured the overlooked player who's still showing up. The coach caught between results and relationships. The leader who's craving clarity in a chaotic world. We saw the parents sacrificing quietly in the background. The young athlete chasing a dream. And the veteran who's still learning. This book is for all of them. This book is for you.

This moment is your moment. It is not about us but about the spark we hope this book lights inside you. A call to lead with soul, not status. To train with purpose, not pressure. To influence not with noise, but with presence. We believe the world doesn't need more winners; it needs more people who win with truth.

This book does not hold all the answers, but we do believe it is a compass. A compass grounded in real life and in tested principles. In the unwavering belief that character is the real scoreboard and how you lead matters far more than what you say.

Our ask is simple: Don't just finish this book. Live it. Make it your own. Let the principles grow with you and within you. Bring them to your team. Your family. Your business. Your classroom. Let them be the language of how you train, lead, love, and show up in this world. When they get tested, as all truths eventually do, we hope you'll remember pressure reveals, not defines.

Because if there's anything we've learned, it's this: the ball still doesn't lie. And neither will your life if you lead with purpose.

We're honored to walk this path with you.

Let's keep playing forward!

Rafa & Joey

ABOUT THE AUTHORS

Rafa Amaya

Rafa is what happens when talent meets purpose and refuses to let go. A former professional player turned licensed pro coach, and trusted advisor to clubs, academies, and federations, Rafa adds soul and structure to *The Ball Never Lies*. His life's work exemplifies the ideas outlined in this book: principles learned through years of repetition, failure, triumph, and leadership under pressure.

Born in Bogotá, Colombia and raised in the United States, Rafa's journey with the game began with grit and imagination. He developed his skills not in pristine academies, but on blacktops, park fields, and community spaces that demanded creativity and passion. Rafa rose swiftly thanks to the support of his family and coaches who saw more than talent in his heart, discipline, and hunger. He was named New York City High School Player of the Year in 1983 before going on to star as a Division I athlete at Long Island University (LIU) on a Pelé scholarship. But that was only the beginning.

Rafa's professional playing career carried him across borders and cultures from Major League Soccer to the Colombian First Division, and to prestigious clubs in Latin America and Asia. In a sport that breaks many down, Rafa adapted, competed, and excelled. However, he did not simply accumulate experiences; he assimilated them. Rafa learned what worked and what didn't on foreign terrain, under various coaches, and in unfamiliar systems. He also understood why leadership, both on and off the field, was more important than anything else.

He took those lessons and built something bigger.

After hanging up his boots, Rafa didn't walk away, instead he stepped up. With top-tier coaching credentials and an unwavering commitment to player development, he became a professional coach and a system builder. He advises national federations on player pipelines, shapes technical direction at elite youth academies, and creates programs that extend far beyond the scoreboard. His frameworks focus on awareness, tactical intelligence, emotional discipline, and values-based decision-making. He helps players see more than just the next pass; he helps them realize who they are becoming as they play the game they enjoy.

And that's the true power of Rafa's contribution to this book. He does not speak in theory. His insights stem from thousands of hours spent teaching, listening, losing, and lifting. He works with national team hopefuls as well as inner-city youth who only have a dream. He leads player evaluations, program conversions, and coach education sessions that alter entire cultures. Rafa brings the same sincerity and intention to every situation he encounters.

His gift is connecting people, not only with players, but also with purpose and performance.

Each of the 11 principles in *The Ball Never Lies* bears Rafa's imprint. These aren't catchy phrases or playbook clichés. They are lived truths. They show how Rafa trains, coaches, and develops trust in locker rooms. He continues to lead with quiet strength in boardrooms and on the training ground. His words will ground the reader, whether you're a youth coach, a professional athlete, a sports psychologist, or a corporate team leader.

Because Rafa has lived it all: pressure, politics, promise, and potential of soccer at all levels.

His comprehensive mastery of the game lends credibility to his voice. Rafa is more than simply a former pro player and active pro coach; he's a father and grandpa who is now witnessing new generations discover the sport. And through them, he is reminded every day that soccer is more than just winning; it is about becoming. About playing with clarity. Leading with conviction. And living in alignment.

So, Rafa's writings about presence, pressure, and preparation are not abstract. It's muscle memory. And when he writes about vision, value, and resilience, it is not based on theory. It comes from fire.

In *The Ball Never Lies*, Rafa provides a mirror and a compass. A reflection of where you are, and a path to where you want to go, regardless of your age, gender, skill level, or position. His experience is a gift. His insights are guidance. And his life teaches us that when purpose drives performance, the results follow.

Rafa's voice in this book is a masterclass for every player looking to improve, every coach looking to do things correctly, and every leader looking to succeed without sacrificing their soul. Because he's not only teaching the game. He is teaching what the game teaches us. And it is the truth. Because *The Ball Never Lies*.

Joey Flores aka Bati

Joey is a globally recognized entrepreneur, leadership strategist, and social impact architect whose work sits at the intersection of purpose, identity, and performance. For decades, he has worked in a variety of capacities with national federations, professional clubs, elite academies, universities, grassroots non-profits, and corporate boards, providing a distinct blend of soul and strategy. His voice in *The Ball Never Lies* provides readers not just insights into the game, but a masterclass in how to lead with conviction when no one is looking.

He is a dual citizen of the United States and Guatemala, and he comes from a multicultural background that includes Italian, Spanish, and Irish roots. He has a degree in International Business from Texas Lutheran University (TLU) and an International MBA from St. Mary's University. His work, which has been recognized by The United States Department of State, The Rockefeller Foundation, and *The Wall Street Journal,* has established him as a thought leader who not only participates in global systems but also helps to rethink them.

But before the accolades and global boardrooms, Joey was a collegiate soccer player with a talent, a work ethic, and a challenge. The problem wasn't with his performance. It was his presence. A presence that intimidated the wrong person in authority.

As an undergraduate student-athlete at TLU, Joey faced one of the most challenging trials of his playing career, not from an opponent on the field, but from a head coach in his locker room. This English coach directed him with humiliation and cruelty, rather than intelligence and empowerment. Joey was subjected to repeated British-style degradation for motives of ego rather than effort. The kind that erodes. To disgrace. To silence. To break.

Whereas others would have snapped, transferred, or quit, Joey stayed, not out of ego, but out of loyalty to his teammates. The team was stacked. There was no shortage of talent, and talent always respects talent. His teammates knew it. They saw the situation clearly. They recognized the politics at play and the quiet strength it took to rise above them.

They called it out. They called him *Bati,* a nickname given in honor of Gabriel Batistuta, the legendary Argentine striker known for his power, precision, and presence. But it wasn't just about the boots. It was about the backbone. About showing up, holding steady, and proving that real leadership doesn't always wear the captain's armband. Sometimes, it wears silence like armor and loyalty like a badge.

His is not a sob story, it's a powerful one. It's the reality in many locker rooms. While others sought stats and All-American honors, aided by self-serving gatekeepers, Joey was forced to pursue something even more challenging: resilience and respect. During the NCAA National Tournament, he was playing a completely different game, one that would not garner him any public recognition but would later provide him with the tools to walk into rooms where those same stat-sheet heroes never reached.

Because, let's be honest, not every talented player gets the story they deserve. There are countless unrecorded losses, players benched by politics, hushed by fragile egos, and driven out by gatekeepers protecting their own insecurities.

Over time, the truth came to light; the same English head coach, who once wielded power to his advantage, was humiliated when he lost his position, title, and place in the game. Meanwhile, Joey's impact grew, and he now stands as proof that legacy is defined by impact, not by accolades. And impact comes from changing the system, not by playing it.

In full circle fashion, a former teammate of Joey's from that same era named Eddie was later hired to lead the very program they once bled for together as players. Not long after, Joey's younger brother, Jimmy, joined the staff, helping reshape the culture from within. What was once a source of disgrace for Joey became a springboard for greater goals.

And Joey didn't simply rise, he evolved.

He utilized hardship to fuel his efforts off the field, becoming a coach's coach and a strategic advisor in rooms where soccer meets global systems. He now sits at tables with executives from federations, professional leagues, universities, amateur clubs, and grassroots non-profits, not only discussing the business side of the game, but also influencing how it's governed, marketed, funded, and grown. His expertise include branding, logistics, international strategy, and business development. And in those rooms, his presence represents every player that has been disregarded, every voice that has been unfairly silenced.

The Ball Never Lies is not a concept for Joey. It is a code. Forged by humiliation. Transformed into leadership. Sharpened through truth.

What about the gift for you, the reader?

You now have those lessons. You get the blueprint, without needing to bleed the same way. You benefit from the experience of someone who not only survived but also continues to improve the system. That's the win. That's the actual scoreboard. Because *The Ball Never Lies*, nor does the life you construct with honesty.

ACKNOWLEDGMENTS

When we reflect on the path that led to the creation of *The Ball Never Lies*, we are filled with gratitude for every person, lesson, and stretch of the journey that shaped this project. This book is both a reflection on personal experiences and a tribute to the numerous people who influence our thinking, play, and purpose.

To Our Readers,

Thank you for approaching these pages with curiosity, openness, and compassion. You are the reason this book exists. Whether you're a player, coach, mentor, parent, or other type of leader, your willingness to participate in this work enhances the meaning of every word. We wrote this book to help sharpen your mindset, deepen your presence, and elevate your impact. Thank you for choosing to step into the arena with us. You are now part of the movement.

To Our Families,

Thank you for being the foundation beneath our feet and the driving force behind our endeavors. This book was created through your sacrifices, shaped by your stories, and fortified by your unwavering love.

To our parents and grandparents, thank you for the sleepless nights, whispered prayers, quiet pride, and loud support. You created us brick by brick, with values that were greater than any trophy. You taught us to lead without being applauded, to care unconditionally, and to fight for something bigger than ourselves.

To our children, grandkids, and future generations, you are our compass and cause. This book was written with you in mind. We are passing on everything we have learned and experienced to you. May you inherit our hustle as much as our hopes. Not only do we tell our tales, but we also show our strength.

Thank you, Amaya Family and Flores Family, for becoming our first team. You taught us how to win with dignity, lose gracefully, and always show up with heart. Every page is embellished with your wisdom. Every principle reflects your example.

This is not only our book. It's yours too.

To Our Mentors and Coaches,

From the fields of the United States, Guatemala, Colombia, and beyond to locker rooms, schools, boardrooms, and back again, you demonstrated how to compete with honor while growing in humility. You taught us the importance of timing, rhythm, presence, and preparation. You shaped not only our methods, but also our character. What you instilled in us has shaped who we are.

To Our Friends and Challengers,

Thank you to both those who supported us and those who opposed us. We had teammates who trusted us. Friends who checked on us. And absolutely, the critics who sharpened our focus. You strengthened the message. You made us sharper. For that, we are grateful.

To Every Kid Still Dreaming

To those training alone. To those with big hearts and quiet voices. To those trying to turn pain into purpose. We see you. We were you. We wrote this book for you. May it offer you the words we needed when we were coming up.

A Final Word

The Ball Never Lies is more than just a title. It's the truth. A compass. A call. This book was written to honor the beautiful game, and the life lessons it continues to teach us. If even one page helps you breathe a little deeper, lead more authentically, or live with greater conviction, then every rep was worthwhile.

With respect, love, and gratitude,

Rafa Amaya & Joey Flores aka Bati